HEALTH & EDUCATION IN NIGERIA

THE PAST, PRESENT & FUTURE

G.E UDDIN (ED.)

Health and Education in Nigeria: The Past, Present and Future

Copyright © 2022 Godwin Enaholo Uddin & Contributors

Godwin Enaholo Uddin

Department of Economics

School of Management and Social Sciences

Pan-Atlantic University, Lagos, Nigeria

ISBN: 9798392946631

All rights reserved. No part of this publication may be reproduced or distributed in any form or by any means, or stored in a data base or retrieval system, without written permission.

This publication is designed to provide accurate and authoritative information in regard to the subject matter covered. It is published under the express understanding that any decision or action you take as a result of reading this book must be based on professional consultation and will be at your sole risk.

The views and opinions expressed in this book are the authors' own and the facts are as reported by them.

Harmony Publishing
Plot 8, Providence Street, Opposite Halifield School, Lekki Phase 1, Lagos, Nigeria.

+2347032212481

publish@harmonypublishing.com.ng

ACKNOWLEDGEMENT

The Editor and Contributors express their gratitude to God who inspires people, and thank the reviewers for making this publication possible.

NOTES ON CONTRIBUTORS

Temitope Racheal Aremu holds a M.Sc. in Economics from the University of Lagos, Nigeria. Her research interests are in development economics.

Kingsley Monday Oserei holds a B.Sc. and M.Sc. in Economics from the University of Lagos, Nigeria. He previously worked at Alpha Morgan Capital, and Nigerian Economic Summit Group (NESG). His research areas are in public sector economics.

Godwin Enaholo Uddin is a member of faculty at the School of Management and Social Sciences, Pan-Atlantic University, Lagos, Nigeria, and also a member of United Nations Educational, Scientific, and Cultural Organization (UNESCO) Inclusive Policy Lab. More so, he is a member of the American Economic Association, a member of the Nigerian Economic Society, an Associate Member of the Institute of Strategic Management, Nigeria, and a Project Management Professional. Prior to joining the faculty at Pan-Atlantic University, Lagos, Nigeria, he worked with Megasea Industries Limited, SuperGeeks Nigeria Limited and Pearlmutual Consulting Limited. ORCID: http://orcid.org/0000-0003-3055-770X.

CONTENTS

Acknowledgement iii

Notes on Contributors v

List of Tables viii

List of Figures ix

Introduction 1

Government Expenditure at Crossroads 3

Primary Health Care and Inclusive Growth 57

Concluding Thoughts 81

LIST OF TABLES

Table 1.1: Federal Expenditure on Education and Health in Nigeria, 1985 – 2014 (₦' million)

Table 1.2: Government's Commitment to Education and Health

Table 1.3: Empirical Evidence on Poverty Reduction / Education / Health Outcomes

Table 1.4: Depiction of the Search Approach Executed

Table 1.1A: Gross Enrolment Ratio (%), 1996 – 2013

Table 1.2A: School Enrolment, 1996 – 2016 and School Age Population, 2017 (in Million)

Table 1.3A: Performance in Ordinary Level (O' Level) Exams, 2008 – 2012

LIST OF FIGURES

Figure 1.1: Federal Expenditure on Education and Health in Nigeria, 1985 – 2014 (₦ million)

Figure 1.2: Government's Commitment to Education and Health (% of total spending)

Figure 1.3: Infants Receiving Three Doses of Hepatitis B Vaccine (%)

Figure 1.4: Under-five Mortality Rate (per 1000 live births)

Figure 1.5: Maternal Mortality Rate (per 100,000 live births)

Figure 1.6: Life Expectancy at Birth (Years)

Figure 1.7: Government Expenditure on Health, Total (% of GDP)

Figure 1.8: School Enrollment, 1996 – 2016 (in millions)

Figure 1.9: Adult Literacy Rate (%)

Figure 1.10: Government Expenditure on Education, Total (% of Total Expenditure)

Figure 2.1: Primary Health Care Provision Framework

Figure 2.2: Triple Pathways of Health Spending Implications

INTRODUCTION

Narratives and or sayings about the realities of the health and education subsectors in Nigeria are obviously no news. Still, as these affect the lowly daily experience of the country's inhabitants, the concern for improved welfare and pathways to address the prevailing inequities remain germane.

This text thereof attempt to make in one piece, a documentary re-statement of the times and efforts relative to the nation's health and education subsectors, for continued appreciation by all stakeholders for the future, and in bid to inform current perspective(s) and prevalent policy directions. Nevertheless, due, appropriate, and concerted opinion(s) are also shared for interested enthusiasts in on-going and future empirical investigations related to the considered subsectors.

This short piece of two (seemingly connected) chapters consists as follows: the first chapter details a time-path discourse of issues and developments in and related to the subsectors considered, that is, the health as well as the education sectors respectively, with mild and or implicit suggestions related to action(s) for the future, while the second chapter makes a succinct discourse, though with bias for the heath sector, on a much thought pathway(s) to improving the welfare of the country's citizenry through and with improvements in the nation's health sector. The last section of this piece presents some concluding thoughts.

GOVERNMENT EXPENDITURE AT CROSSROADS

GOVERNMENT EXPENDITURE AT CROSSROADS

Temitope Racheal Aremu, and Godwin Enaholo Uddin

T. R. Aremu
Department of Economics, Faculty of Social Sciences,
University of Lagos, Nigeria
e-mail: temmyracheal2010@yahoo.com

G. E. Uddin (Corresponding author)
School of Management and Social Sciences,
Pan-Atlantic University, Lagos, Nigeria;
Veronica Adeleke School of Social Sciences,
Babcock University, Ilishan-Remo, Ogun State, Nigeria
e-mail: guddin@pau.edu.ng

This work appreciates the mentorship of Amihai Glazer, Professor of Economics at the Department of Economics, University of California, Irvine, CA, USA, and Margaret Abiola Loto, Professor of Economics at the Department of Economics, University of Lagos, Nigeria.

CHAPTER SUMMARY

The appeal for equitable provision for all is no news. Whereas, in Nigeria, the disparity between level of attention to income distribution and response to citizenry's plight, in varied respects, remain a concern. Thereof, the purpose of this article was to review literature, on budgetary allocations vis-à-vis health and education outcomes in Nigeria, alongside usage of descriptive analytics. Literature/statistics show education and health sectors' outcomes have not improved significantly for the period under consideration. Also, sectoral spending(s) were below standard. Thus, the government is encouraged to overhaul the country's education and health sectors to identify/address constraints for increased budgetary allocation to be reasonable.

Keywords: Budgetary Allocations, Government Expenditure, Health, Education, Nigeria

JEL Classification: H11; H51; H52

1.0 INTRODUCTION

Even in contemporary times, budgetary allocation concerns have informed partly the focus of welfare economists (Navarro and Skirbekk 2018). This is to the extent that, the recurring gap between needs evaluation/assessments of sectors of a country's economy (or of supposed indigent communities) and manner of project implementation in the form of fiscal responses to the problem of inequities in income distribution in world economies, more especially in Less-Developed Countries (LDCs), are becoming more evident (OECD 2014; Glazer and Proost, 2020).

Also, the deployment of resources by the government in LDCs is recounted to be increasingly *less-optimal* (or *less-efficient*)[1]. Therefore, such is a vacuum that appeals for more informed fiscal intervention procedure(s) and contributory participation of social sector players / social entrepreneurs / non-governmental organizations, for reasons including lack of political will (Piketty 2015; Davies, Lluberas and Shorrocks 2017).

Whereas, in as much as successive governments in Nigeria have been known to dutifully exclaim commitment to equitable distribution of income, all in a bid to assure the citizens of the possible enjoyment of the dividends of democracy (Oserei and Uddin 2019), still the increasing

---

[1] This is synonymous with the notion that the intended objectives of certain fiscal expenditures may not be fully realized (Osuji and Nwani 2020).

disparity between the level of the government's attention to income distribution and her response to the (obvious) plight of the citizenry, in varied respects, remains a concern (Kress, Su, and Wang 2016; Okoli et al. 2016). Nonetheless, the main asset of the poor is their labour, and policies that favour investment in education and health are noted to foster improvement in productivity, socio-economic development, and quality of lives of the people (Barenberg, Basu and Soylu, 2016; AFDB, OECD and UNDP 2017).

Besides, Taiwo, Soyele, and Ndubuizu (2014) had argued the efficacy and or effectiveness of the health sector, and by extension the education sector, to depend on the extent to which they meet the health care needs, educational needs, and interests of varying categories of people in the economy, most especially people that are vulnerable with low income, the destitute, the less privileged and the likes found in the society who are in dire need for improvement in their health and educational status. More so, popular appeal to institutions had been for the equitable provision of basic amenities for all and sundry (or for all persons). This, however, is expressed to be in the manner irrespective of their social class or income purchasing power (Terai and Glazer, 2015; Oserei and Uddin 2019; Adam and Nwaogwugwu 2020; Oke and Mohammed 2021).

Thus, the purpose of this article to undertake a succinct review of literature, and this specifically on budgetary allocations vis-à-vis health and education outcomes in

Nigeria, but in particular reference to the years 1985 and 2015[2]. In other words, a pertinent research question sought to be answered here is: have the varied levels of budgetary allocations improved health and education outcomes in Nigeria for the period 1985 till 2015? Precisely, this study considers the duration following the adoption of the Structural Adjustment Programme (SAP), the inception of the democratic regime from the year 1999, and before the onward implementation of the Sustainable Development Goals (SDGs) in Nigeria.

Several related studies had considered empirical procedure(s) to examine the efficacy of government spending (and or interventions or policies) on poverty reduction (and or educational / health (sectoral) outcomes) but with mixed conclusions[3] (Osundina, Ebere, and Osundina 2014; Ude and Ekesiobi 2014; Barenberg et al. 2016; David 2018; Onakoya, Johnson and Ogundajo 2019; Anetor, Esho and Verhoef 2020; etc.), while here presented in this article is a recall of the government spending vis-à-vis health and education outcomes' axiom and a proposition of possible future direction(s) respective to the Nigerian case in policy making

---

[2] Notably, for the sake of prudence and or to avoid possible wrongly understood / fast-judgmental assertions, the authors did not make an evaluation beyond 2015 as respectively would be inclusive of the present federal administration in Nigeria due to her inauguration in 2015 / wielding of power since 2015, re-election in 2019, and her tenure still to elapse in 2023 despite the already spent 7-year timeline in implementation of the Sustainable Development Goals (SDGs) in the country.

[3] Here, we acknowledge that the consideration of specifics in pre-existing empirical published literature could inform a pathway for another empirical investigation (or journey) in face of mixed conclusions. Also, one can appreciate in the Concluding Remarks section, i.e. in Section 6, some suggestions for further research.

and implementation through conceptual narrative and or descriptive analytics, a notable contribution to pre-existing literature (Osundina et al. 2014; Ude and Ekesiobi 2014; Kress et al. 2016; etc.). Additionally, Pluye and Hong (2014), Squires et al. (2014), Anselmi, Lagarde, and Hanson (2015), Ferrari (2015), Pare et al. (2015), Barlow et al. (2017), Liao et al. (2017), Ibrahim et al. (2019), Snyder, (2019), Padhan and Prabheesh (2021), Page et al. (2021), etc. had proposed conceptual narrative / meta-narrative review procedure as an alternative research method adoptable herein as way forward for contextual (rather than generalized) usage of these mixed findings, and this through thematic review of relevant literature can help highlight salient notions raised, but possibly lost due to analytical rigour/emphasis, and give the answer to a research question. The foregoing thereof informs the motivation of this study, and the gap(s) in literature this article attempt to close.

Following the introductory section, in Section 2, the stylized facts are reiterated. Section 3 details the literature review, Section 4 contains the methodology, and Section 5 presents the discussions. Section 6 concludes.

2.0 STYLIZED FACTS

From Table 1.1 as follows and Figure 1.1, government recurrent spending in both the education and health sectors was significantly higher than her capital spending in all the years, and such therefore implies that the government did not invest sufficiently in these sectors since capital spending represents a real investment in the sectors.

Furthermore, in terms of the government's commitment to education and health sectors perceivable through the percentage of each sector's spending to the total government spending (Table 1.2), it is observed that the government showed little commitment to the health sector relatively. As shown, in 2000, only 2.6% of government spending was devoted to the health sector. However, it rose to 6.2% in 2002 which was the highest ever attained within the period under study. This is far below what is required given the nature of the Nigerian economy, concerning the prevalence of diseases, and the low level of service in health care facilities.

Also, important to note, the government's commitment to the education sector fluctuated between 1985 and 2014 (Figure 1.2). Between the years 1985 to 2001, a steady fall and rise (shock) was recorded with a peak of 10.8% in 2002. It decreased to 6.5% in 2003 and stays within that range till 2006 when it rose to 8.5%. It declined to 5.2% in 2009 and increased to 7.9% in 2011. It fell to 6.6% in 2013 and rose to 7.2% in 2014. This situation is not encouraging given the increasing population and needs for work-place suited graduates, research, and development in the country. By extension, when viewed against the United Nations' benchmark for developing countries of spending about 26% of the annual budget on education, it is apparent Nigeria needs to invest more in education.

Table 1.1: Federal expenditure on education and health in Nigeria, 1985-2014 (₦' million)

Year	Education Recurrent Spending	Education Capital Spending	Total Education Spending	Health Recurrent Spending	Health Capital Spending	Total Health Spending
1985	669.5	180.7	850.2	167.7	56.2	223.9
1986	652.8	442	1,094.8	279.2	81.2	360.4
1987	514.4	139.1	653.5	166.9	69.5	236.4
1988	802.3	281.8	1,084.1	260	183.2	443.2
1989	1,719.90	221.9	1,941.8	326.6	126	452.6
1990	1,962.60	331.7	2,294.3	401.1	257	658.1
1991	1,265.10	289.1	1,554.2	619.4	137.6	757
1992	1,676.30	384.1	2,060.4	837.4	188	1,025.4
1993	6,436.10	1,563	7,999.1	2,331.60	352.9	2,684.5
1994	7,878.10	2,405.70	10,283.8	2,066.80	961.00	3,027.8
1995	9,421.30	3,307.40	12,728.7	3,335.70	1,725.20	5,060.9
1996	12,136.00	3,215.80	15,351.8	3,192.00	1,659.50	4,851.5

1997	12,136.00	3,808.00	1,5944	3,179.20	2,623.80	5,803	
1998	3,928.30	12,793.00	16721.3	4,860.50	7,123.80	11,984.3	
1999	23,047.20	8,516.60	31563.8	8,793.20	7,386.80	16,180	
2000	44,225.50	23,342.60	67568.1	11,612.60	6,569.20	18,181.8	
2001	39,884.60	19,860	59744.6	24,523.50	20,128.00	44,651.5	
2002	100,240.20	9,215	109455.2	50,563.20	12,608	63,171.2	
2003	64,755.90	14,680.20	79436.1	33,254.50	6,431.00	39,685.5	
2004	72,217.90	21,550.00	93767.9	33,377.40	26,410.00	59,787.4	
2005	92,594.70	27,440.80	120035.5	50,032.80	21,652.60	71,685.4	
2006	129,421.90	35,791.80	165213.7	67,550.20	38,039.80	105,590	
2007	137,478.26	48,293.51	185771.8	71,228.99	51,171.01	122,400	
2008	163,977.47	48,800	212,777.5	98,219.319	97,200	195,419.32	
2009	137,116	43,400	180,516	90,200	52,500	142,700	
2010	170,800	87,900	258,700	99,100	35,000	134,100	
2011	335,800	35,400	371,200	231,800	39,500	271,300	
2012	348,400	61,650	410,050	197,900	37,250	235,150	

| 2013 | 390,424.8456 | 48,525 | 438,949.8 | 179,986.94 | 38,375 | 218,361.93 |
| 2014 | 311,119.1823 | 55,087.5 | 366,206.7 | 194,964.78 | 37,812.5 | 232,777.28 |

Source: CBN Statistical Bulletin 2014; Author

Figure 1.1: Federal expenditure on education and health in Nigeria, 1985-2014 (₦' million)

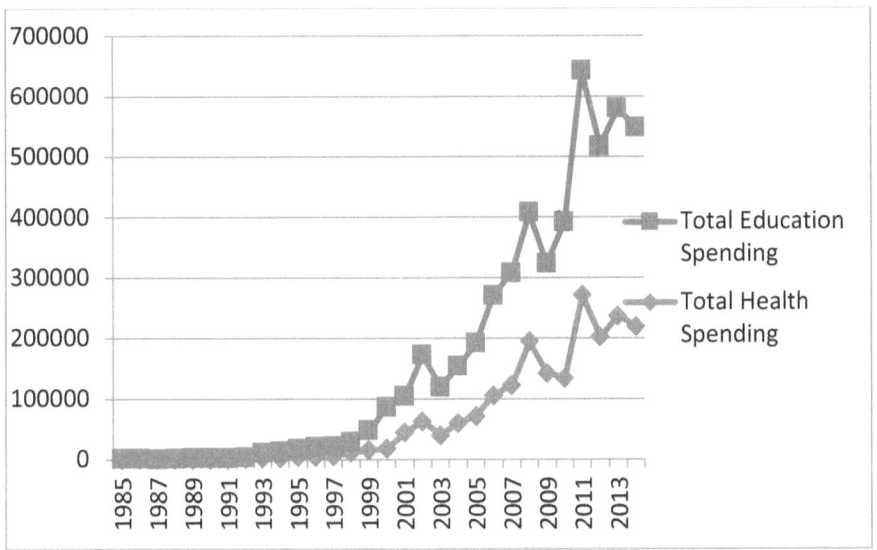

Source: CBN Statistical Bulletin 2014; Authors

Table 1.2: Government's commitment to education and health

Year	Total Education Spending (₦'Million)	Total Health Spending (₦'Million)	Total Spending (₦'Million)	Education % of Total	Health % of Total
1985	850.2	223.9	13,041.1	6.519389	1.7168797
1986	1,094.8	360.4	16,223.7	6.748152	2.2214415

1987	653.5	236.4	22,018.7	2.967932	1.0736329
1988	1,084.1	443.2	27,749.5	3.906737	1.5971459
1989	1,941.8	452.6	41,028.3	4.732831	1.103141
1990	2,294.3	658.1	60,268.2	3.806817	1.09195
1991	1,554.2	757	66,584.4	2.33418	1.1369
1992	2,060.4	1,025.4	92,797.4	2.220321	1.10499
1993	7,999.1	2,684.5	191,228.9	4.182997	1.40382
1994	10,283.8	3,027.8	160,893.2	6.391693	1.88187
1995	12,728.7	5,060.9	248,768.1	5.116693	2.03438
1996	15,351.8	4,851.5	337,217.6	4.552491	1.43869
1997	15,944	5,803	428,215.2	3.723362	1.35516
1998	16,721.3	11,984.3	487,113.4	3.432733	2.46027
1999	31,563.8	16,180	947,690	3.330604	1.70731
2000	67,568.1	18,181.8	701,059.4	9.637999	2.59347
2001	59,744.6	44,651.5	1,018,025.6	5.868674	4.38609
2002	109,455.2	63,171.2	1,018,155.8	10.75034	6.20447
2003	79,436.1	39,685.5	1,225,965.9	6.479471	3.23708
2004	93,767.9	59,787.4	1,426,200	6.574667	4.19208
2005	120,035.5	71,685.4	1,822,100	6.587756	3.93422
2006	165,213.7	105,590	1,938,002.5	8.524948	5.44839
2007	185,771.77	122,400	2,450,896.7	7.579747	4.99409
2008	212,800	195,400	3,240,819.6	6.56624	6.02934

2009	180,500	142,700	3,452,990.8	5.227352	4.13265
2010	258,700	134,100	4,194,576.5	6.167488	3.19699
2011	371,200	271,300	4,712,062	7.877655	5.75756
2012	314,950	202,700	4,605,390.5	6.838725	4.40136
2013	343,075	237,000	5,185,318.5	6.616276	4.5706
2014	329,012.5	219,850	4,578,065	7.186715	4.80225

Source: CBN Statistical Bulletin 2014; Authors

Figure 1.2: Government's commitment to education and health (% of total spending)

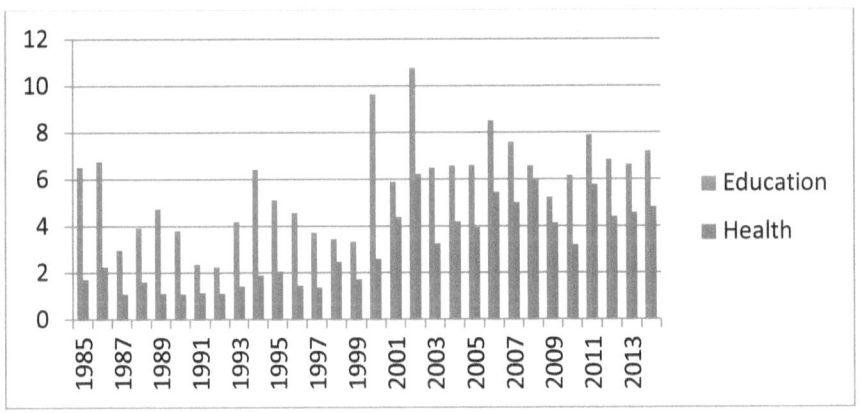

Source: CBN Statistical Bulletin 2014; Authors

3.0 LITERATURE REVIEW

3.1 Conceptual issues

Education has to do with the refinement of "the whole person" which includes intellectual, character, and mental development (Healy 2014). The simple importance of education is to empower individuals with knowledge, and the ability to apply that knowledge (Pavlova 2017). The significance of the education sector in human development can never be overemphasized (Reimers 2017). Several studies have pointed out the positive social impact of education, thus buttressing arguments in favour of government interventions in the education sector (Elumah and Shobayo 2017; Bulut 2018; Akinyoade 2019; etc.).

On the other hand, health they say is wealth; therefore, the first wealth of any nation is her health. More so, since the burden of diseases can slow economic growth, the linkages of health to poverty eradication and long-term economic growth are strong (Adeyi 2016; Oserei and Uddin 2019; Adam and Nwaogwugwu 2020).

Consequently, education and health are important tools to empower poor people and overcome exclusion based on gender, location, and other correlates of poverty. A number of the Millennium Development Goals (MDGs) were directly related to education and health, although the overarching goal is the eradication of extreme poverty, the development of the human person through education and health is key (Kaur and Singh 2014; NBS 2015; Nyandekwe, Kokoma and Nzayirambaho 2018). Thence, we may recall that, a mild reference to poverty, seemingly relates to the level of (adult) educational literacy inadequacies as well as the level of the varied (health) morbidity and mortality situations, and not only in term of income impoverishments (Barenberg, Basu and Soylu, 2016; AFDB, OECD and UNDP 2017).

Government spending, through budgetary outlay, refers to the outflow of resources from government to other sectors of the economy, whether requited or unrequited. It comprises both capital and recurrent spending. Capital spending would mean payments for non-financial assets used in the production process for more than one year (i.e., expenses on capital projects like buildings, electricity generation, etc.) while recurrent spending would mean payments for non-repayable transactions within one year (i.e., expenses on administration - wages, salaries, etc.) (Onalo, Lizam, and Kaseri 2016; Alqadi and Ismail 2019). Total government spending on education as a percentage of GDP thereof include both the recurrent and capital spending on education by local, regional, and national governments for a given year, while Total government spending on health as a percentage of GDP is the recurrent and capital spending on health by local, regional, and national governments for a given year (Ukwueze 2015). One of the main purposes of government is notably to provide infrastructural facilities, but the provision and maintenance of these facilities require a substantial amount of spending (Jibir and Aluthge 2019).

3.2 Theoretical framework

The protagonist emphasis on the role of government for social provision in the economic literature is renowned attributable to the seminal work of Wagner (1893), which attests of public sector growth to result due to reasons including an increase in distributive functions of the state (Magazzino, Giolli, and Mele 2015; Ukwueze 2015; Jibir and Aluthge 2019; Osuji and Nwani 2020). Furthermore, Musgrave and Musgrave (1989) assert this growth in government spending to be the case as a result of increasing demand for public goods and services such as education, health, etc. (Terai and Glazer, 2015; Oserei and Uddin 2019). Thus, government efforts to meet the citizenry's aspirations for a better quality of life is much anticipated (Keho 2016; Afonso and Alves 2017).

3.3 Empirical review

In summary, from the literature, it is evident that the effect of varied interventions or policies on poverty reduction have been mixed, in the same vein as the relations between government spending, amidst others, and education/health (sectoral) outcomes. Nevertheless, this study considers the Nigerian case with a recall of the government spending vis-à-vis health and education outcomes' axiom and thereby proposes possible future direction(s) in policy making and implementation through conceptual narrative and or descriptive analytics, a notable contribution to pre-existing literature (Osundina et al. 2014; Ude and Ekesiobi 2014; Kress et al. 2016; etc.).

Table 1.3 summarizes the published literature (or peer-reviewed / scientific documents) on the efficacy of government spending (and or interventions or policies) on poverty reduction (and or educational / health (sectoral) outcomes) in tabular form as follows:

Table 1.3: Empirical evidence on poverty reduction/education/health outcomes

Author(s)	Country / Countries	Sample Period/Details	Methodology	Results/Conclusion of the Study
Yiadom et al. (2021)	42 African economies	2011 to 2018	Dynamic panel regression	The study attests of the efficacy of institutions associated with financial inclusion for poverty reduction effect.
Nyamutswa (2021)	Zimbabwe	Primary data from 398 observations	Stratified random sampling technique, with data analyzed using Stata	The research showed socioeconomic variables effect on health outcome, among which education had

			Version 11	positive influence while distance to primary health centre and personal income had negative influence.
Abdul-Mumuni (2021)	Ghana	Ghana Living Standards Survey round six (GLSS 6) data	Poisson regression	The article reported the positive effect of increase in household income on child's health outcome.
Anetor, Esho, and Verhoef (2020)	29 Sub-Saharan African countries	1990 to 2017	FGLS technique	The study concluded that foreign direct investment and official development assistance harm poverty reduction.
Akyuz et al. (2020)	26 Latin American countries	1980 to 2014	Bootstrap panel Granger causality test	The findings indicated that Granger causality existed between trade openness and life expectancy.
Rezapour et al. (2019)	105 countries with moderate and high-level income	2000 to 2015	Panel OLS	The findings from the study indicated that an increase in public health expenditure led to increase in life expectancy and decrease in infant and under-five mortality rates.
Onakoya, Johnson, and Ogundajo (2019)	21 African countries	2005 to 2014	Pooled panel regression, Co-integration test	The findings showed that foreign direct investment and inflation rate had a positive relationship with

					the human development index, while the exchange rate and trade openness were negatively related to the poverty level.
Nketiah-Amponsah (2019)	46 sub-Saharan African countries	1996 to 2015		A combination of descriptive analytics, and Panel OLS	Health expenditure per capita was found to exert a significant impact on all three health outcomes considered.
Farooq et al. (2019)	47 Organization of Islamic Cooperation (OIC) member countries	1991 to 2017		GMM	The results revealed that trade openness, public health expenditures, public education expenditures, and economic growth were positively and significantly correlated with life expectancy.
Novignon et al. (2018)	42 sub-Saharan African countries	1995 to 2013		Panel OLS and GMM	The results showed a positive and significant relationship between trade openness and life expectancy, negative and significant relationship between trade openness and infant mortality rate and negative relationship between trade openness and under-five

					mortality rate.
Jawadi et al. (2018)	12 countries in the MENA (Middle East and North Africa) region	1970 to 2015	Panel OLS		The study found that trade openness has a positive effect on health in the MENA region as it reduces the infant mortality rate, and boosts life expectancy.
Headey (2018)	308 middle income and low income countries	1990s to 2000s	Panel OLS and IV approach		The findings attest that increases in food prices are associated with reductions in poverty.
David (2018)	Nigeria	1980 to 2016	ARDL, Co-integration, and Granger causality		The results concluded the existence of a long-run relationship between infant mortality and government health expenditure.
Herzer (2017)	74 developed and developing countries	1960 to 2010	Panel OLS		The findings showed a positive relationship between life expectancy and trade openness, and negative relationship between infant mortality and trade openness.
Arthur and Oaikhenan (2017)	40 Sub-Saharan African countries	1995 to 2014	Panel OLS		The findings indicated that health expenditure has a significant effect on health outcomes in SSA, reducing mortality rates and improving life

					expectancy at birth.
Barenberg et al. (2016)	31 Indian States and union territories	1983-1984 to 2011-2012	Panel OLS, 2SLS, and IV estimation strategy		The findings suggest public health expenditure reduces infant mortality rate.
Ashiabi et al. (2016)	40 Sub-Saharan African countries	2000 to 2010	Panel OLS		The results indicated that public health expenditure was inversely and significantly related to infant and under-five mortality rates in SSA.
Ude and Ekesiobi (2014)	Nigeria	1980 to 2012	OLS		The study revealed per capita health spending has no significant effect on infant mortality rate and neonatal mortality rate, but the under-five mortality rate was significantly affected.
Osundina, Ebere and Osundina (2014)	Nigeria	1970 to 2012	VECM		The results showed the effect of government spending on education and health was insignificantly negative and positive respectively.

Notes: OLS-ordinary least squares, VECM-vector error correction model, ARDL-autoregressive distributed lag, FGLS-Feasible Generalized Least Squares, GMM-generalized method of moments, 2SLS-two stage least squares, IV-instrumental variable

Source: Authors

4.0 METHODOLOGY

In consonance with the purpose to make a conceptual narrative / meta-narrative – a type of review of literature – as a research method for this review article (Burton 2014; Pluye and Hong 2014; Squires et al. 2014; Ferrari 2015; Pare et al. 2015; Barlow et al. 2017; Liao et al. 2017; Ibrahim et al. 2019; Snyder 2019; Page et al. 2021; etc.), a three-fold process to consider in a succinct manner pre-existing literature (or peer-reviewed / scientific articles) on budgetary allocation vis-à-vis health and education outcomes in Nigeria was adopted / implemented. The stages were as follows.

First, authors resorted to the search for (and or exploration) of relevant literature delimited, out of convenience, to 70 articles amidst others, and these sourced from reputed databases (or depositories) hosted by the following institutions (Table 1.4) – a search approach made using phrases such as *health sector outcomes in Nigeria, education sector outcomes in Nigeria, health sector policy in Nigeria, education sector policy in Nigeria, budgetary allocation / government expenditure on education in Nigeria, budgetary allocation / government expenditure on health in Nigeria.*

Table 1.4: Depiction of the Search Approach Executed

Institutions whom databases / depositories were accessed	Number of relevant articles sourced
Academic Journals, Nigeria	3
American Economic Association – AEA, Nashville, Tennessee, USA	2
Central Bank of Nigeria – CBN, Abuja, Nigeria	2
Google Scholar, Google LLC, Mountain View, California, USA	18
International Bank for Reconstruction and Development – IBRD / World Bank, Washington, D. C., United States of America (USA)	4
National Bureau of Statistics – NBS, Abuja, Nigeria	2
Organization for Economic Cooperation and Development – OECD, Paris, France	2
Routledge – Taylor & Francis Group, Informa UK Limited (Taylor & Francis Online), Oxfordshire, United Kingdom	22
ScienceDirect, Elsevier B. V	5
Springer Online, Springer Nature, Switzerland AG	4
United Nations Economic Commission for Africa – UNECA, Addis Ababa, Ethiopia	2
Wiley Online Library, John Wiley & Sons Inc., New Jersey, USA	4

Source: Authors

Second, an alignment to renowned articles, a careful concise consideration of the relevant literature, and overall to consult the literature on the subject matter – *government budget allocation, health care (and policy) in Nigeria, education policy in Nigeria, etc.* was made with salient themes drawn, and as thoughts, perspectives, and or implications established from the consulted literature so as to proffer informed submission(s) as therein presented in this article. These themes thereof which served as the 'focal lens' in touch with the relevant literature include *government and budgetary allocation, government healthcare provision in Nigeria, government education provision in Nigeria.*

Third, the last stage – the use of the literature, which suffices not simply as a recitation / repetition of the consulted literature but as a snowball (or snowballing) presentation of the survey of the (relevant) literature, or otherwise a documentation of echoes of findings of the present review commensurate to answer the research question.

To conclude this section, it is prudent to reiterate that evidence of conceptual narrative(s) / meta-narrative(s) procedure – a type of review of literature – as a research method[4] for review articles, and as used for this research could be appreciated in works such as Burton (2014), Pluye

---

[4] This seemingly new but emerging (qualitative) research method adopted herein had been somewhat uncommon (or rarely used), as a stand-alone research method in economic literature, whereas the same method relatively becoming popular in the pure (and allied) sciences, humanities, and management sciences (Burton 2014; Pluye and Hong 2014; Squires et al. 2014; Ferrari 2015; Pare et al. 2015; Barlow et al. 2017; Liao et al. 2017; Ibrahim et al. 2019; Snyder 2019; Uddin et al. 2020; Imhanzenobe 2021; Padhan and Prabheesh 2021; etc.).

and Hong (2014), Squires et al. (2014), Ferrari (2015), Pare et al. (2015), Barlow et al. (2017), Liao et al. (2017), Ibrahim et al. (2019), Snyder (2019), Uddin et al. (2020), Imhanzenobe (2021), Padhan and Prabheesh (2021), etc.

5.0 DISCUSSIONS

5.1 Preliminary notes

Over the years, successive Nigerian governments recognized the importance of human capital formation in the development process and have embarked on various programmes and projects which led to the establishment of educational institutions and health centres throughout the country. However, in the late 1970s and early 1980s, federal government spending grew substantially resulting in a fiscal crisis, inflation, and heavy borrowings. Subsequently, through the austerity measures adopted in 1982 and the structural adjustment programme introduced in 1986, the country attempted to bring down fiscal deficits as part of its stabilization and adjustment programmes, often by reducing public spending on an across-the-board basis. These reductions resulted in unprecedented economic and social costs as human resources development was neglected with adverse long-term development consequences (Shuaib, Enatto, and Hakeem 2015).

5.2 The Government and Health Sector in Nigeria

In the mid-Eighties, the Nigerian health sector recorded some successes, but this success was not sustained. Among other things, routine immunization coverage increased and this led to a reduction in infant and child mortality rates. Unfortunately, there has been a downward trend in health development since 1993 (Figure 1.3). Research has also shown that most of Nigeria's disease burden is due to preventable diseases, and poverty is one of the causes of these problems (Adeyi 2016; Kress et al. 2016; Oserei and Uddin 2019; Okoebor 2021; etc.).

Under-five mortality per 1,000 and maternal mortality per 100,000 live births as of 1999 in Nigeria was 138 and 840 respectively, compared to sub-Saharan Africa's average of 130 and 646 (Okoli et al. 2016). Still in Nigeria, as of 2015 (Figures 1.4 and 1.5), not much improvement has been recorded (see also Kress et al. 2016 for 1990 – 2013 trend graph), compared to selected economies and Africa average performance (World Health Statistics 2016). Also, life expectancy at birth[5] had not much improved over the years (Figure 1.6).

---

[5] The authors although acknowledge that life expectancy at birth, in years, as a health status indicator, has been criticized as a less accurate measure of population health relative to mortality rates, due to measurement issues. Still, it is argued that life expectancy at birth, been a broader measure of population health with mortality, morbidity, disability, and other health indicators considered in its measurement, reflects how long, on average, people will live, based upon a given set of age-specific death rates (Novignon et al. 2015; Novignon et al. 2018; Nketiah-Amponsah 2019).

Figure 1.3: Infants receiving three doses of hepatitis b vaccine (%)

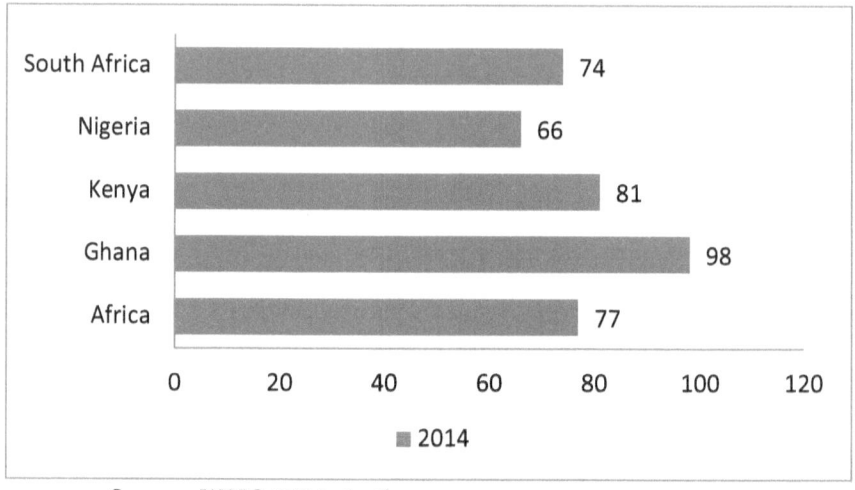

Source: WHO 2016; Authors

Figure 1.4: Under-five mortality rate (per 1,000 live births)

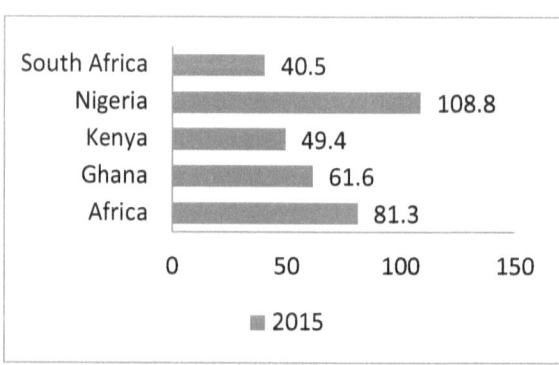

Source: WHO 2016; Authors

Figure 1.5: Maternal mortality rate (per 100,000 live births)

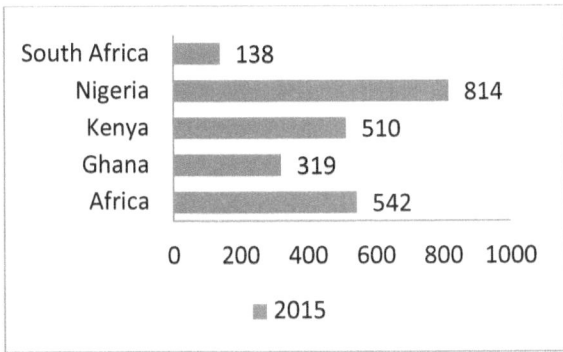

Source: WHO 2016; Authors

Figure 1.6: Life expectancy at birth (years)

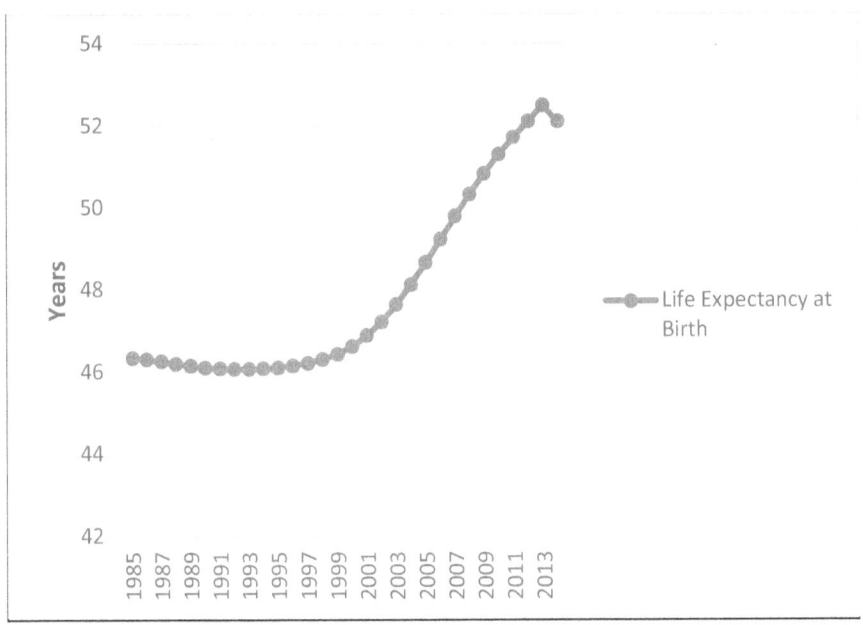

Source: WDI 2018; Authors

Health spending per capita in Nigeria as of 1999 stood at US$23, while as of 2009 it was estimated at US$69, below the sub-Saharan Africa average (SSA) of US$76, although $34 is recommended internationally. Private expenditures were estimated to be over 70% of total health expenditure, with most of it coming from out-of-pocket expenditures despite the endemic nature of poverty (Uzochukwu et al. 2015). Government spending on health was 2.5% of Gross Domestic Product (GDP) on average between 1994 and 1998, and also from 2009 till 2011 it accounted for 5.4% of the total government budget and 0.7% of the GDP on average compared to selected economies (Figure 1.7), while in 2012, 6% of aggregate government spending was proposed as government spending on health but of note also was the disclosure in 2004 that there is no broad-based health financing strategy (Budget Office of the Federation 2014).

Figure 1.7: Government expenditure on health, total (% of GDP)

Country	1994-1998	2009-2011
South Africa		6.9
Nigeria	0.7	2.5
Ghana		3.9
Africa		4

Source: Budget Office of the Federation 2014; Authors

More so, as in a like manner that these figures indicate government spending on health in Nigeria is far short of the African Union's Abuja declaration of 2001 (which appropriate 15% of the government's spending on health), WHO (2014) and Kress et al. (2016) had reported that over the years since the inception of democracy in 1999 only 3.2% of the aggregate government spending on average was devoted to health. While still, the proportion of recurrent expenditure on health increased between 2009 and 2014, but that of capital expenditure on health decreased between 2009 and 2014. Thus far, in most states of the federation, the proportion of states' and local government areas' budgets allocated to health remains below 15%. However, there has been significant improvement in funding for some diseases/programs e.g., immunization, AIDS, tuberculosis, malaria (Budget Office of the Federation 2014).

We may also recall Uzochukwu et al. (2015) who reported Nigeria's social services provision had not improved significantly despite increased budgetary allocations. With emphasis, the slow pace of rehabilitation of basic facilities, and the high incidence of industrial actions in the health sector were attested to have hampered service delivery by the key institutions and departments. Specifically, in the health sector as of 2001, the performance was mixed. The budgetary allocation to the sector which rose to about 5 percent, from about 3 percent the previous year, enabled repeated house-to-house visits by medical personnel to immunize children against the six childhood diseases, and the efforts made contributed to the overall rate immunization rising from 72.7 percent in 2000 to 74.6 percent in 2001, but other health indicators including population per physician, population per hospital bed, and population per nursing staff deteriorated owing largely to prolonged industrial action.

To end this section, Okoli et al. (2016) had reiterated that funding for the health sector had been declining over time, and such height of underfunding explains much of the poor health status of Nigerians despite the obvious need for massive public investments for the rehabilitation of health facilities.

5.3 The Government and Education Sector in Nigeria

The Universal Primary Education (re-launched in 1999 as Universal Basic Education (UBE) Scheme) has been a stated priority of every Nigerian government since its introduction in the 1970s, but the actual commitment of the different governments to the scheme varied substantially. More so, as the economic problems encountered also contributed to the difficulties experienced in its implementation, successful implementation depended on the availability of adequate resources, the sharing of responsibility amongst different levels of government, and the level of community, and of student participation. In recognition of the need for greater participation of stakeholders in the implementation of the scheme, previous governments passed legislations that spell out the responsibilities of different levels of government and those of various stakeholders, and other initiatives including the reinstatement of the National Primary Education Commission and other management structures from 1993 and basic steps taken to promote increased access to education since 1990 (Akinyoade 2019).

Nonetheless, a detailed survey, measuring attainment in three competencies – literacy, numeracy, and life skills – was commissioned by the Federal Government of Nigeria in partnership with United Nations International Children's Emergency Fund (UNICEF) and the United Nations Educational, Scientific and Cultural Organization (UNESCO) in 1997 - confirmed that the quality of education offered at the primary school level was low. Although, the pupils performed better in life skills learned through the curriculum as well as those that were acquired outside the school environment, performance in literacy was the worst amongst the three competencies measured (Akinyoade 2019).

From available data, as of 1996, education statistics in Nigeria showed that out of the 21 million children of school-going age and 7.2 million young persons aged 12-14years, about 68 percent enrolment rate was observed for children in primary schools while below 40 percent enrolment rate was recorded for pupils at the secondary school level. Tertiary enrolment was 4 percent (Table 1.1A in Appendix A). The low number of students in the tertiary school was related due to poor spending per student in tertiary schools, which cumulatively amounted to 9.8% of Gross National Product (GNP) (World Bank 2017). More so as illustrated and shown (Figure 1.8 and Tables 1.1A, 1.2A in Appendix A), enrolment across the levels of education grew over time relatively, in same manner as the school-age population by education level (FME 2017; UNESCO 2017; World Bank 2017; WDI 2018).

Figure 1.8: School enrolment, 1996 - 2016 (in million)

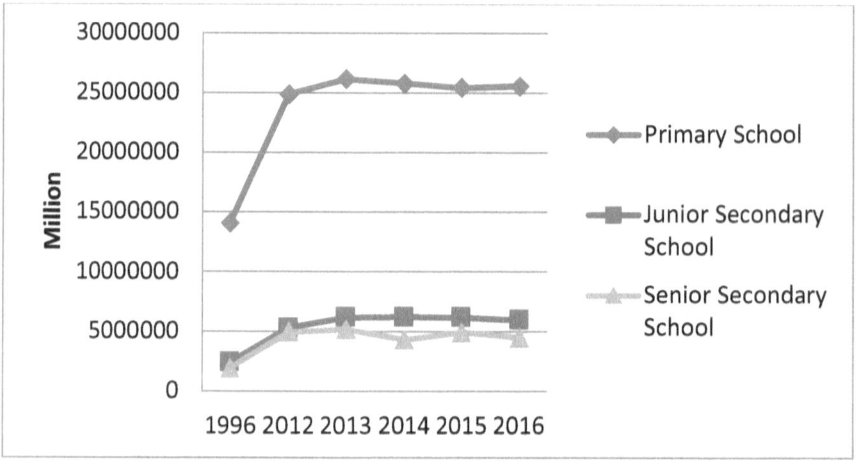

Source: FME 2017; Authors

Whereas, on the World Economic Forum's Global Competitiveness Index Report, 2011-2012, Nigeria was ranked 140th out of 144 countries in primary education enrolment and 120th out of 144 in secondary education enrolment. Also, the deplorable state of the Nigerian education system was evident in students' poor performance in WASSCE and NECO (Table 1.3A in Appendix A) (Akinyoade 2019), as well as in the level of adult literacy rate attained over the years (Figure 1.9) (WDI 2018). The tertiary institutions as noted likewise have had their challenges which ranged from inadequate learning facilities, unavailability of modern learning equipment, poor funding, frequent strikes, unhealthy politics, etc. (Elumah and Shobayo 2017).

In addition, despite the importance of educational institutions, Nigeria spends almost an insignificant proportion of her financial resources on education relative to other economies (Figures 1.10a - d). It was a mere 0.6 percent of the total expenditure in 1970, with the highest proportion of 10.8 percent in 1976. This fell to a mere 2.3 percent in 1991, before it increased to about 10 percent in 2000 (CBN 2014; World Bank 2017). The United Nations recommends that 26 percent of government budget be devoted to education, but total education spending as a proportion of the annual fiscal budget in Nigeria had been below 10 percent since 2003 (CBN 2014).

Figure 1.9: Adult literacy rate (%)

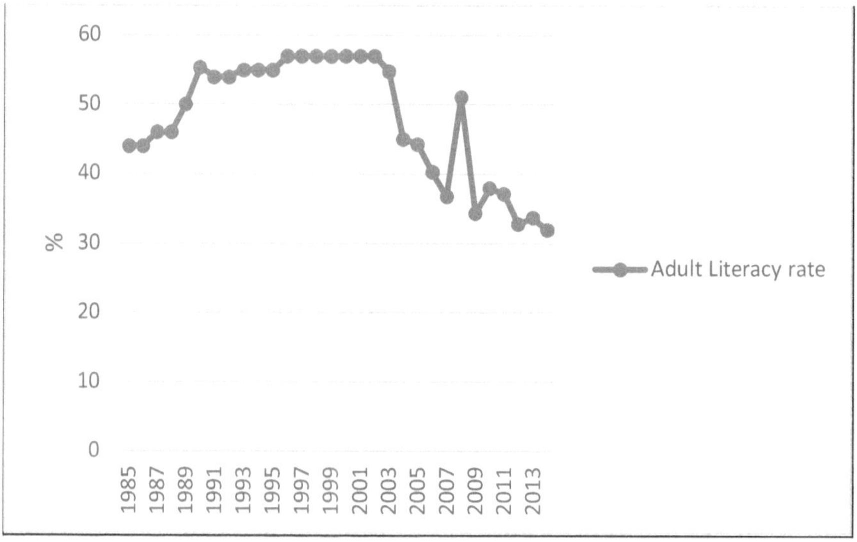

Source: WDI 2018; Authors

Figure 1.10: Government expenditure on education, total (% of total expenditure)

(a)

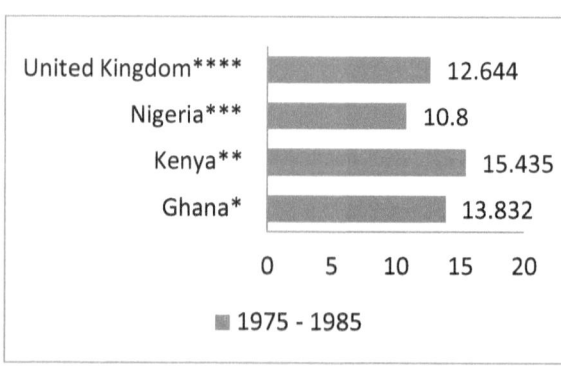

Source: World Bank 2017; Authors
*1982; ** 1985; ***1976; ****1981

(b)

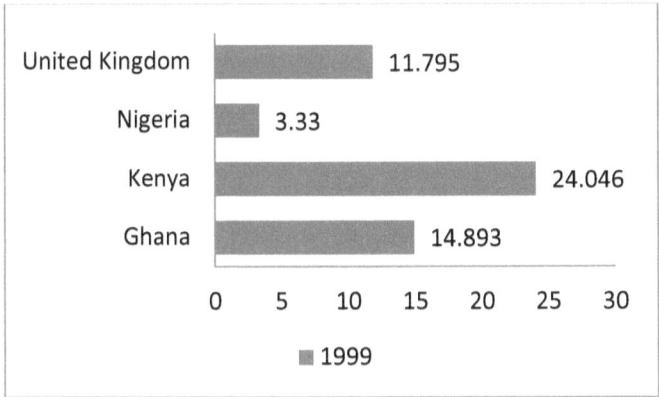

Source: World Bank 2017; Authors

(c)

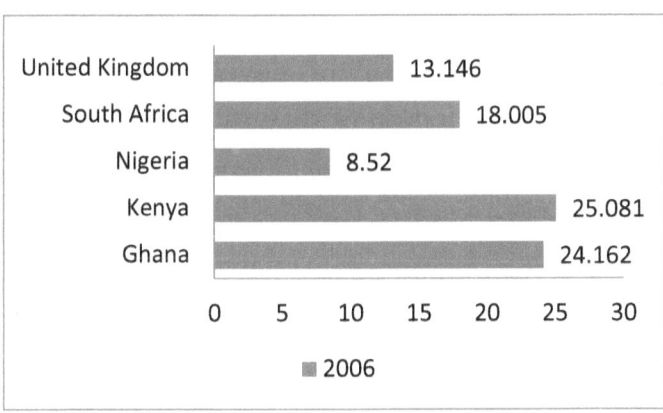

Source: CBN 2014; World Bank 2017; Authors

(d)

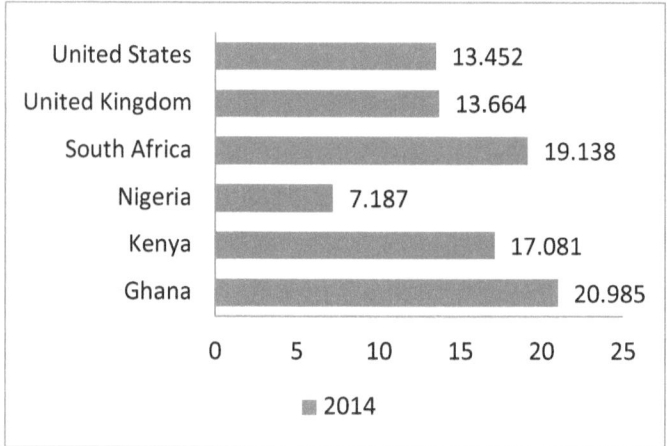

Source: CBN 2014; World Bank 2017; Authors

The education sector as well was reported to have received an enhanced budgetary allocation in the year 2000, which accounted for about 10 percent of the government budget. Such thereof enabled rehabilitation of schools under the UBE program and contributed to modest improvements, as enrolment in both primary and secondary schools increased from 24.9 million and 6.4 million respectively in 2000 to 25.9 million and 6.7 million respectively in 2001. Other education system indicators including pupil/teacher ratio for both primary and secondary levels however deteriorated slightly from 54 and 41 in 2000 to 56 and 45 respectively in 2001 (CBN 2014; Akinyoade 2019).

Lastly, UNECA (2015) noted that Nigeria confronts two main problems in human resource development: unemployment among the educated youths and the dwindling federal budgetary allocations to educational institutions. The report relayed that the growing unemployment among recent graduates, particularly at the tertiary level, stems in part from the mismatch between educational output and requirements of the labour market, while the quality and relevance of education have declined as academic resources, whether faculty or equipment and facilities have become in increasingly short supply. More so, attempts by the government to create more employment through public works programmes have only made a limited impact. With a growing national population, the situation is understood to be challenging as enrolments have outpaced budgetary allocations. Thus, the declining funding for education poses a major obstacle to solving the problem of poor quality in education, and unemployment among educated youths.

6.0 CONCLUDING REMARKS

In conclusion, this study purposeful to undertake a succinct review of literature on budgetary allocation vis-à-vis health and education outcomes in Nigeria, but particularly between the years 1985 and 2015, and with descriptive analytics has shown education and health sectors' outcomes in Nigeria to have not improved significantly for the period under consideration. Also, the education and health sectoral outcomes were evident to be poor, with respective sectoral spending below the international standard, before the onward implementation of the SDGs in Nigeria.

Thence, in line with previous studies such as Authur and Oaikhenan (2017), Onakoya et al. (2019), Oserei and Uddin (2019), Anetor et al. (2020), Osuji and Nwani (2020), etc., the findings from this review thereof argue more the emphasis (or rationale) for the Nigerian government to ensure prudent implementation of the SDGs going forward, and which include addressing the inequities in income distribution (or directed efforts towards poverty reduction) and eradicating the country's citizenry's (or inhabitants') limitations to improved educational and health status.

Moreover, as a suggestion for future research, a later consideration of a post-2015 scenario analysis and or a study beyond year 2015 but similar to the context here presented for the Nigerian case could be made (or investigated), and such most suitable following the tenure expiration of the present federal administration in Nigeria which is scheduled as of year 2023. A similar consideration may also be undertaken for other developing economies, even in the Sub-Saharan African region.

Finally, it is recommended that the government in Nigeria should overhaul the country's education and health sectors to identify and address constraints that undermine efficiency, to make propositions for increased budgetary allocation reasonable.

7.0 DECLARATIONS

7.1 Funding

The authors declare no research funding.

7.2 Conflict of interests

The authors declare no conflict of interest.

REFERENCES

Abdul-Mumuni A (2021) The effect of household income on child welfare clinic attendance in Ghana. *African Journal of Economic and Sustainable Development* 8(1): 1-17

Adam VY, Nwaogwugwu JC (2020) Availability of personnel, facilities and services in primary health care centres in a local government area in Benin City, Nigeria. *Annals of Clinical and Biomedical Research* 1(111): 29 – 33

Adeyi O (2016) Health system in Nigeria: From underperformance to measured optimism. *Health Systems & Reforms* 2(4), 285 – 289

AFDB, OECD, UNDP (2017) Africa Economic Outlook (https://www.afdb.org/fileadmin/uploads/afdb/Documents/Publications/AEO_2017_Report_Full_English.pdf)

Afonso A, Alves J (2017) Reconsidering Wagner's law: Evidence from the functions of the government. *Applied Economics Letters* 24(5): 346 - 350

Akinyoade A (2019) Nigeria: Education, labour market, migration. African Studies Centre Leiden

Akyuz M, Karul C, Demir I (2020) Life expectancy and trade openness: Causality in Latin America. *International Journal of Social Economics* 47(10): 1265-1281

Alqadi M, Ismail S (2019) Government spending and economic growth: Contemporary literature review. *Journal of Global Economics* 7(4): 1-4

Anetor FO, Esho E, Verhoef G (2020) The impact of foreign direct investment, foreign aid, and trade on poverty reduction: Evidence from sub-Saharan African countries. *Cogent Economics & Finance* 8(1),

Anselmi L, Lagarde M, Hanson K (2015) Equity in the allocation of public sector financial resources in low- and middle-income countries: A systematic literature review. *Health Policy and Planning* 30, 528 – 545.

Arthur E, Oaikhenan HE (2017) The effects of health expenditure on health outcomes in Sub-Saharan Africa (SSA). *African Development Review* 29(3): 524–525

Ashiabi N, Nketiah-Amponsah E, Senadza B (2016) The effect of health expenditure on selected maternal and child health outcomes in Sub Saharan Africa. *International Journal of Social Economics* 43(12): 1386–1399

Barenberg, AJ, Basu D, Soylu C (2016) The effect of public health expenditure on infant mortality: Evidence from a panel of Indian states, 1983-1984 to 2011-2012. *The Journal of Development Studies* 53(10): 1765-1784

Barlow P, McKee M, Basu S, Stuckler D (2017) The health impact of trade and investment agreements: A quantitative systematic review and network co-citation analysis. *Global Health* 13, 13

Budget Office of the Federation – Federal Republic of Nigeria (2014) *2014 Budget*

Bulut H (2018) Government intervention in higher education: A theoretical approach. *The Online Journal of Quality in Higher Education* 5(3): 42-48

Burton LD (2014) Doing research (part 1): Finding a problem to investigate. *Journal of Research on Christian Education* 23(1): 1 – 4

Central Bank of Nigeria (2014) *Statistical bulletin*.

David J (2018) Infant mortality and public health expenditure in Nigeria: Empirical explanation of the nexus. *Timisoara Journal of Economics and Business* 11(2): 149 – 164

Davies JB, Lluberas R, Shorrocks AF (2017) Estimating the level and distribution of global wealth, 2000 – 2014. *Review of Income and Wealth* 63, 731- 759

Elumah LO, Shobayo PB (2017) Effect of expenditures on education, human capital development, and economic growth in Nigeria. *Nile Journal of Business and Economics* 3(5): 40 – 50

Farooq F, Yusop Z, Chaudhry IS (2019) How do trade openness and public expenditures affect health status in OIC member countries? An empirical analysis. *Pakistan Journal of Commerce and Social Sciences* 13(4): 1041-1056

Federal Ministry of Education – FME (2017) *Nigeria education indicators 2016*

Ferrari R (2015) Writing narrative style literature reviews. *Medical Writing* 24(4): 230 – 235

Glazer A, Proost S (2020) Benefits to the majority from universal service. *International Tax and Public Finance* 27(2): 391-408

Headey DD (2018) Food prices and poverty. *The World Bank Economic Review* 32(3): 676-691

Healy C (2014) Development education through drama in education. In: R Dolan (ed.) *Pathways to innovation and development in education: A collection of invited essays.*

Maynooth University Department of Education, July 2014 (http://mural.maynoothuniversity.ie/5800/1/RD_Pathways.pdf)

Herzer D (2017) The long-run relationship between trade and population health: Evidence from five decades. *The World Economy* 40(2): 462-487

Ibrahim A, Abdalla SM, Jafer M, Abdelgadir J, de Vries N (2019) Child labour and health: A systematic literature review of the impacts of child labour on child's health in low-and middle-income countries. *Journal of Public Health* 41(1): 18-26

Imhanzenobe, J. (2021) Impact of globalization on work ethics: A review of existing literature. *Journal of Economics and International Finance* 13(3): 127-135

Jawadi F, Gouddi SE, Ftiti Z, Kacem A (2018) Assessing the effect of trade openness on health in the MENA region: A panel data analysis. *Open Economies Review* 29, 469-479

Jibir A, Aluthge C (2019) Modelling the determinants of government expenditure in Nigeria. *Cogent Economics and Finance* 7:1 1620154, DOI: 10.1080/23322039.2019.1620154

Kaur A, Singh K (2014) Role of teacher education in the achievement of MDGs. *International Journal of Evaluation and Research in Education* 3(2): 125-132

Keho Y (2016) Testing Wagner's law in the presence of structural changes: New evidence from six African countries (1960 – 2013). *International Journal of Economics and Financial Issues* 6(1): 1 - 6

Kress DH, Su Y, Wang H (2016) Assessment of primary health care system performance in Nigeria: Using the primary health care performance indicator conceptual framework. *Health System and Reforms* 2(4), 302 – 318

Liao Y, Deschamps F, Loures E de FR, Ramos LFP (2017) Past, present, and future of Industry 4.0 – a systematic literature review and research agenda proposal. *International Journal of Production Research* 55(12), 3609 - 3629

Magazzino C, Giolli L, Mele M (2015) Wagner's law and Peacock and Wiseman's displacement effect in European Union countries: A panel data study. *International Journal of Economics and Financial Issues* 5(3): 812 – 819

National Bureau of Statistics – NBS (2015) *The millennium development goals performance tracking survey 2015 report* (http://www.ng.undp.org/content/nigeria/en/home/libr ary/mdg/NigeriaMDGsSurveyReport2015.html) (accessed 29 December 2020).

Navarro J, Skirbekk V (2018) *Income inequality and religion globally 1970 – 2050.* Scripta Instituti Donneriani Aboensis 28, 175 - 199

Nketiah-Amponsah E (2019) The impact of health expenditures on health outcomes in sub-Saharan Africa. *Journal of Developing Societies* 35(1): 134-152

Novignon J, Nonvignon J, Arthur E (2015) Health status and labour force participation in sub-Saharan Africa: A dynamic panel data analysis. *African Development Review* 27(1): 14–26

Novignon J, Atakorah YB, Djossou GN (2018) How does the health sector benefit from trade openness? Evidence from sub-Saharan Africa. *African Development Review* 30(2): 135–148

Nyamutswa TO (2021) Social determinants of health in rural Zimbabwe: An econometric data analysis. *African Journal of Economic and Sustainable Development* 8(2): 167-184

Nyandekwe M, Kokoma JB, Nzayirambaho M (2018) The health-related millennium development goals (MDGs) 2015: Rwanda performance and contributing factors. *Pan African Medical Journal* 31:56 [doi: 10.11604/pamj.2018.31.56.11018]

Oke DM, Mohammed IA (2021) Budgetary institutional quality and the cyclical nature of fiscal policy in oil exporting economies. *Interdisciplinary Journal of Economics and Business Law* 10(1): 44 – 66

Okoebor R (2021) Challenges of the Nigerian health care system and the fight against coronavirus. *Academia Letters*, Article 854 https://doi.org/10.20935/AL854

Okoli U, Eze-Ajoku E, Oludipe M, Spieker N, Ekezie W, Ohiri K (2016) Improving quality of care in primary health-care facilities in rural Nigeria: Successes and challenges, *Health Services Research and Managerial Epidemiology* 3 (https://doi.org/10.1177/2333392816662581)

Onakoya A, Johnson B, Ogundajo G (2019) Poverty and trade liberalization: Empirical evidence from 21 African countries. *Economic Research* 32(1): 635 – 656

Onalo U, Lizam M, Kaseri A (2016) Government expenditure and the economy: The Nigeria perspective. *Archives of Current Research International* 4(1): 1-12

Organization for Economic Cooperation and Development - OECD (2014) *Pisa for development – capacity needs assessment.* OECD / World Bank

Oserei K, Uddin G (2019) The myth and reality of government expenditure on primary health care in Nigeria: Way forward to inclusive growth. MPRA Paper No. 99094

Osuji E, Nwani SE (2020) Achieving sustainable development goals: Does government expenditure framework matter? *International Journal of Management, Economics and Social Sciences* 9(3): 131 - 160

Osundina CK, Ebere C, Osundina OA (2014) Disaggregated government spending on infrastructure and poverty reduction in Nigeria. *Global Journal of Human-Social Science* 14(5)

Padhan R, Prabheesh KP (2021) The economics of COVID-19 pandemic: A survey. *Economic Analysis and Policy* 70, 220 – 237

Page, M. J., McKenzie, J. E., Bossuyt, P. M., Boutron, I., Hoffmann, T. C., Mulrow, C. D., et al. (2021). The PRISMA 2020 statement: An updated guideline for reporting systematic reviews. *BMJ* 372:n71. doi: 10.1136/bmj.n71

Pare G, Trudel MC, Jaana M, Kitsiou S (2015) Synthesizing information systems knowledge: A typology of literature reviews. *Information and Management* 52(2), 183 - 199

Pavlova M (2017) *Two pathways, one destination – TVET for a sustainable future*. UNESCO International Centre for Technical and Vocational Education and Training (UNESCO-UNEVOC) and Griffith Institute for Educational Research, Australia (https://unevoc.unesco.org/conference/susdev/TwoPathways_FinalReport.pdf)

Piketty T (2015) About capital in the twenty-first century. *The American Economic Review* 105(5): 48 - 53

Pluye P, Hong QN (2014) Combining the power of stories and the power of numbers: mixed methods research and mixed studies reviews. *Annual Review of Public Health* 35, 29 – 45

Reimers FM (2017) Rediscovering the cosmopolitan moral purpose of education. In *Meaningful Education in Times of Uncertainty: A Collection of Essay*. The Brookings Institution, August 2017 (https://www.brookings.edu/wp-content/uploads/2017/07/meaningful-education-times-uncertainty-essays.pdf)

Rezapour A, Mousavi A, Lotfi F, Soleimani MM, Alipour S (2019) The effects of health expenditure on health outcomes based on the classification of public health expenditure: A panel data approach. *Shiraz e-med journal* 20(12): e88526

Shuaib IM, Enatto AL, Hakeem KA (2015) Impact of innovation for the 21st-century educational sector in Nigerian economic growth. *Journal of Education, Society, and Behavioural Science* 9(1): 11 – 21

Snyder H (2019) Literature review as a research methodology: An overview and guidelines. *Journal of Business Research* 104, 333 – 339

Squires A, Finlayson C, Gerchow L, Cimiotti JP, Matthews A, Schwendimann R, Griffiths P, Busse R, Heinen M, Brzostek T, Moreno-Casbas MT, Aiken LH, Sermeus W (2014) Methodological considerations when translating "burnout". *Burnout Research* 1, 59-68

Taiwo OA, Soyele OO, Ndubuizu GU (2014) The pattern of utilization of dental services at federal medical centre, Katsina, Northwest Nigeria. *Sahel Medical Journal* 17(3): 108-11

Terai K, Glazer A (2015) Budgets under delegation. In: T Ihiro, K Terai (eds.) *The political economy of fiscal consolidation in Japan* (pp. 167 – 192), Advances in Japanese Business and Economics, Volume 8, Tokyo: Springer

Uddin GE, Monehin AO, Osuji E (2020) Strengthening Financial System Regulation: The Nigerian Case. *International Journal of Management, Economics and Social Sciences* 9(4): 286-310

Ude DK, Ekesiobi CS (2014) Effect of per capita health spending on child mortality in Nigeria. *International Journal of Innovative Research & Development*, 3(9)

Ukwueze ER (2015) Determinants of the size of public expenditure in Nigeria. *Sage Open* 5(4): 1-8

United Nations Economic Commission for Africa – UNECA (2015) *Economic report on Africa 2015: Industrializing through trade.*

United Nations Educational, Scientific and Cultural Organization – UNESCO Institute of Statistics (2017) *Nigeria: Education system*

Uzochukwu BS, Ughasoro MD, Etiaba E, Okwuosa C, Envuladu E, Onwujekwe OE (2015) Health care financing in Nigeria: Implications for achieving universal health coverage. *Nigerian Journal of Clinical Practice*, 18, 437 - 44

World Bank (2017) Health, nutrition and population statistics, Washington, DC.

World Development Indicators – WDI (2018) *Nigeria – World Bank open data.*

World Health Organization – WHO (2014) *Global health expenditure database*

World Health Organization – WHO (2016) *World health statistics 2016: Monitoring health for the SDGs*

Yiadom EB, Dziwornu RK, Yalley S (2021) Financial inclusion, poverty and growth in Africa: Can institutions help? *African Journal of Economic and Sustainable Development* 8(2): 91-110

APPENDIX A

Table 1.1A: Gross Enrolment Ratio (%), 1996 – 2013

Years	1996	2008	2009	2010	2011	2012	2013
Primary Education	67.15	84.1	85.35	85.07	90.62	92.04	94.07
Secondary Education	30.4	35.37	39.21	44.2	45.54	47.16	56.18
Tertiary Education	4.00	-	-	9.57	10.17	-	-

Source: UNESCO, 2017; World Bank, 2017; WDI, 2018; Authors
* - means data are not available.

Table 1.2A: School Enrolment, 1996 – 2016 and School-Age Population, 2017 (in Million)

Years	1996	2012	2013	2014	2015	2016
Primary School *	14,100,000	24,893,442	26,158,376	25,801,197	25,442,535	25,591,181
Junior Secondary School **	2,400,000	5,277,527	6,168,764	6,203,094	6,180,291	5,968,142

| Senior Secondary School *** | 1,915,200 | 4,934,722 | 5,152,805 | 4,292,489 | 4,910,944 | 4,475,309 |

	Primary	Secondary	Tertiary
School-age population (2017)	31,037,469	25,346,640	15,875,252

Source: FME, 2017; UNESCO, 2017; Authors

* Insurgency in the North East especially in Borno State affected data collection from 2011 to 2015

** Insurgency in the North East especially in Borno State affected data collection from 2013 to 2015

*** Borno State was worst hit in insurgency and such made it difficult to get the enrolment for the years 2014 and 2015

Table 1.3A: Performance in Ordinary Level (O' Level) Exams, 2008 - 2012

Years	2008	2009	2010	2011	2012
Students with five credits in the May/June WASSCE*	23%	26%	24%	31%	39%
The failure rate for NECO	98%	88%	89%	92%	68%

Source: Akinyoade (2019); Authors
* including English and Mathematics

PRIMARY HEALTH CARE AND INCLUSIVE GROWTH

PRIMARY HEALTH CARE AND INCLUSIVE GROWTH

Kingsley Monday Oserei, and Godwin Enaholo Uddin

K. M. Oserei (Corresponding author)
Department of Economics, Faculty of Social Sciences, University of Lagos, Nigeria
e-mail: osereikingsley@yahoo.com

G. E. Uddin
School of Management and Social Sciences, Pan-Atlantic University, Lagos, Nigeria;
Veronica Adeleke School of Social Sciences, Babcock University, Ilishan-Remo, Ogun State, Nigeria
e-mail: guddin@pau.edu.ng

This work appreciates the mentorship of Risikat Oladoyin S. Dauda, Professor of Economics at the Department of Economics, University of Lagos, Nigeria.

CHAPTER SUMMARY

The health sector remains a vital tool for sustainable development of any nation and therefore investment in this sector cannot be overemphasized. This article examines primary health care service provision in Nigeria as well as its relations to be efficacious for inclusive growth. Nonetheless, such efficacy duly was also understood to be limited in three select aspects: funding / financing strategy, personnel / manpower quality and mobilization, and implementation framework. Thus, this article in conclusion attests to the rationale that money spent wisely on capital health expenditure pays off well in both short-run and long-run for individuals, the society and nation at large.

Keywords: Nigeria, Government Expenditure on Health, Primary Health Care, Inclusive Growth

JEL Classification: H0; H5; H51

INTRODUCTION

The health sector is widely acclaimed to be vital for the sustainable development of any nation, and therefore investment in this sector cannot be overemphasized. Also remarkably, government expenditure on primary health centers in Nigeria has notably led to improvement in various areas such as reduction in mortality rates, morbidity and increase in life expectancy rate. (Nixon and Ulmann, 2006; Anyanwu and Erhijakpor, 2009; Novignon, Olakojo and Nonvignon, 2012). However, the efficiency and effectiveness of the health sector is argued to depend on the extent to which it is all-embracing, that is, meeting the health needs and interest of varying categories of people in the economy, most especially people that are vulnerable with low income, the destitute, the less privileged and the likes found in the society who are in dire need for improvement in their health status (Abimbola, 2012; Taiwo, Soyele, and Ndubuizu, 2014). Meeting the needs of such ones as these consequently could help achieve one of the Sustainable Development Goals (SDGs) which is eradicating poverty (AFDB, OECD and UNDP, 2017).

Furthermore, in facilitating human capital development, a vibrant and an all-inclusive health sector is also put forth to be fundamental. Stated differently, policies that favor investment in the health sector is noted to foster improvement in productivity, socioeconomic development, and quality of lives of the people which enables them to be more productive, skillful, and industrious, thereby translating into economic growth (Oluwatobi and Ogunrinola, 2011; AFDB et al, 2017). Whereas, with all or most of the investment in health been derived from the public sector, even so in the case of Nigeria, such questions that may arise include: Could government spending on primary health care be always productive? Could government spending on health always achieve the desired positive result, possibly as well as including inclusive growth?

The financing of the health sector is reiterated also in literature to directly and or indirectly affect per capita income and economic growth. Thus, as economic growth may be defined as the sustained increase in national output overtime, promotion of primary health care financing can lead to increase in human capital through capital accumulation and impact economic growth directly (Saad and KalaKech, 2009). It also improves labour efficiency through increased longevity and reduction in working days due to illness which affects productivity incidentally (Berger and Messer, 2002; Herrera and Pang, 2005; Novignon et al, 2012).

But over the years in Nigeria, while the health sector has been placed on top priority by several administrations, the health care system is still underdeveloped to face the challenges of the 21st century (World Health Organization, 2000; World Health Organization, 2005; Obalum and Fiberesima, 2012; Kress, Su, and Wang, 2016; Okoli, Eze-Ajoku, Oludipe, Spieker, Ekezie and Ohiri, 2016). Besides as of the Nigerian case, the manner which the provision of health services is handled reflects the structure of government. The federal government is responsible for tertiary health care, state governments for secondary health care, and the local governments handle primary health care. Meanwhile, the impact of local government administration on the people with regards to primary health care however still remains a subject of debate. Thus, an effort therefore to respond to the aforementioned concern(s), more particularly as to the Nigerian case, informs the purpose of this article.

CONCEPTUAL ISSUES

The primary health care system is a grass-root approach meant to address the main health problems in both rural and urban centers, by proffering preventive, curative and rehabilitative solution-based health services at an affordable and accessible rate for all individuals (Olise, 2012). More so, the Alma Ata declaration of 1978 defined primary health care as the "essential care based on practical, scientifically sound and socially acceptable methods and technology, made universally accessible to individuals and families in the community through their full participation, and at a cost that the community and country can afford to maintain at every stage of their development in the spirit of self-reliance and self-determination" (WHO-UNICEF, 1978; WHO, 2011; Aigbiremolen et al, 2014).

On the other hand, as the popular form of economic organization for economic progress is of a capitalist orientation, and which obviously since had led for 'side-lined' growth even in contemporary times is de-emphasized, the notion or concept of inclusive growth - a participatory measure in both the development process as well as an encapsulated stake in resulting benefits and all forms of accrued outcome – remains highly upheld either explicitly or implicitly. Any discourse thus about sustainable development as a Post-2015 Agenda draws to mind the issue of realizing inclusive growth (United Nations Department of Economic and Social Affairs, 2015). However, such enviable feat in recent times has more often than not been notably undermined whereby employment provision is not ensured, sectoral imbalance prevails, and particularly when non-participatory development measures are held in high esteem amidst innumerable negative consequences. As a result, such limitation(s) to development especially in developing economies, and of which Nigeria is one, are such that remains a concern.

In a recent conference on sustainable development, economic growth and economic development were opined as not synonymous. Thus, economic development requires sound foundations which are not just inclusive of universal access to education, access to financial services, new technologies and affordable bank loans, gender equality and more equal distribution of resources but also of universal access to health services since all can support economic development.

Investments in infrastructure are notable as vital for economic growth and accessibility and affordability of the services provided is expected to be taken into consideration already when planning these investments. Popular public-private-partnerships are a valued option for financing infrastructure, and a wide funding mix, suitable for each project, could be utilized so that institutions fostering growth may be in a manner that becomes sensitive to the needs of people (United Nations Department of Economic and Social Affairs, 2015).

Inclusive growth talks not just of participation or sharing benefit but also sharing or taking part in outcome(s) i.e. not taking a back-seat approach or role in development process but taking an active part or venturous approach or participatory contribution in the development process. Thus, a framework or milieu offering opportunities, improving people's capabilities as expected by Sen (1985) capabilities approach is such envisaged or such that is germane. An implication here refutes in no manner an appeal for a growth process that means a broad-based growth, a growth process that is all encompassing or a growth process that is all embracing. Hence, the case of social protection, welfare extension services or establishing welfare provision structure complimentary to the capitalist approach in development process are such that are implied factors inherent as necessary in attaining or achieving or engendering inclusive growth.

PERSPECTIVES TO HEALTH CARE PROVISION

The Wagner's Law of Increasing State Activities which argues that there are inherent tendencies for the activities of different layers of a government (such as central and state governments) to increase both intensively and extensively, is one that continually resonate in literature focused on functional relationship between the growth of an economy and the growth of the government activities (Wagner, 1893; Nitti, 1903; Musgrave and Musgrave, 1989; Brown and Jackson, 1990; Bhatia, 2002).

Whereas, Nitti (1903), Musgrave and Musgrave (1989) and Brown and Jackson (1990) had laid bare the traditional functions of the state to include defence, justice, law and order, maintenance of the state and social overheads, but over time the government's interest to enrich the cultural life of the society and to provide social security to the people would accommodate efforts that account for redistributing income and wealth (Brown and Jackson, 1990). Thence, the need to provide and expand the sphere of public goods becomes increasingly recognized, and one of such goods obviously is the provision of health services – of which a possible framework to ensure its sustainable provision and optimum contribution to society's welfare is as illustrated (Figure 2.1) (Bakare and Olubokun, 2011; Kress, Su and Wang, 2016).

However, such general tendency of expanding state activities is reiterated to be of a long term trend, though in the short run financial difficulties could come in the way. Still, by implication therefore in the long run, the desire for development by a progressive people is recounted to always overcome these financial difficulties (Bhatia, 2002; Bakare and Olubokun, 2011).

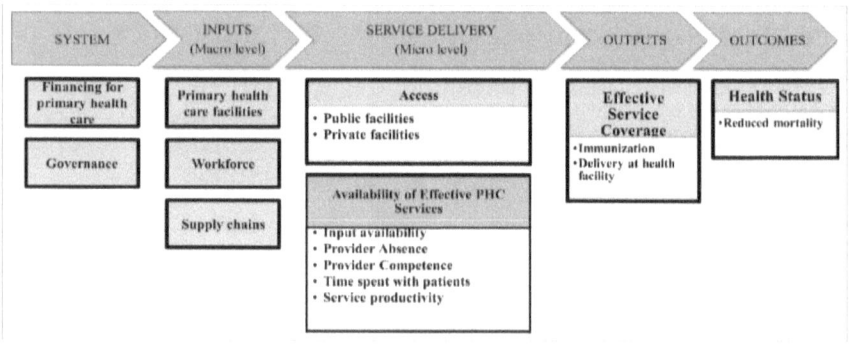

Figure 2.1: Primary Health Care Provision Framework
Source: Kress, Su, and Wang (2016)

It is to this end, in view to engender inclusive growth, that public spending, made apparent from Keynesian macroeconomics, is attested as such which can have a significant impact on economic growth. A rise in government spending is therefore effective in producing some beneficial results (Herrera and Pang, 2005). Thus, expenditure on public health, the amount of capital formation, and labour productivity are anticipated to partially determine the level of economic growth (Ichoku and Fonta, 2006; Odior, 2011).

Public health expenditure is anticipated to have a favorable (and or positive) effect on economic growth, as it is expected that a rise in public health expenditure will enhance the health of the labour force (Filmer and Prittchet, 2007), and thus boost their productivity. In the same vein, it is inevitable that enhanced labour productivity will boost gross national production (Novignon et al, 2012).

SUGGESTION(S) FOR INCLUSIVE GROWTH THROUGH HEALTH CARE PROVISION

Such relationship(s) as highlighted in the preceding section (i.e. section 3), and as expressed in economic literature thus reflect, in our opinion, the tripartite possibilities that government expenditure on health could engender, in a bid to realize inclusive growth especially in developing economies including Nigeria (Figure 2.2). More so, the foregoing is as supported in Saad and Kalakech (2009), Oluwatobi and Ogunrinola (2011), Novignon et al. (2012), and AFDB et al. (2017).

First, the immediate case could result whereby health care institutions are made available or equipped, in first place, to render requisite health care services. Then as a result, same institutions in turn make available to the working-age population or labour force unconditional treatment for their deteriorating health due to work engagements, and their affiliated work organizations empowering them to access health care (often at times with Health Maintenance Organization (HMO) enrollment(s), National Health Insurance Scheme (NHIS) enrollment, etc., as these common nowadays in developing economies including Nigeria).

Second, the medium-term or intermediate case rests on the assumption of the effectiveness of existing health care institutions, that the efficacy of government expenditure on health to engender a sustainable labour force would be in terms of existing health care institutions being ever ready to offer the working-age population opportunities to preserve or maintain their health status. Thus, whereby existing health care institutions effectively provide the working-age population unconditional health care services, and their affiliated work organizations evidently empower them to access health care, such (i.e. government expenditure on health) ultimately could help foster economic growth.

Third, in respect to the distant-time possibility, with government expenditure on health focused on primary health care (PHC) – i.e. particularly providing communal or targeted health services – such would in no small measure promote health care accessibility that is efficacious to counteract basic ailments of the working-age populace, and so reduce their susceptibility to same ailments (or foster health care accessibility which is capable to reduce their morbidity condition and improve their life expectancy). Furthermore as earlier mentioned, on assumption of the effectiveness of health care facilities, whereby existing health care facilities are made ever ready (available and or equipped) to offer the working-age populace opportunities to preserve or maintain their health status and same health care facilities providing same working-age populace unconditional health care services, with their affiliated work organizations evidently empowering them to access health care, the recounted government expenditure on health to engender a sustainable labour force could ultimately help foster economic growth.

Exclusion thereof is recognized of the sect of the country's (working-age) population or labour force not engaged in paid-employment. Thus, consequent to such recognition and the need to proffer appropriate action(s), the demand for health care services by this recognized sect of persons obviously can be at best ensured on basis of social service provision, borne or made feasible by the government and or non-governmental organizations.

Figure 2.2: Triple Pathways of Health Spending Implications
Source: Authors

CONCLUSION

This article demonstrates a beneficial connection between spending on health care and economic growth in line with a priori expectations, similarly applicable to labour power and economic growth. Thence, it would not be out of place to suggest that public expenditure has a crucial connection to any nation's growth and development, as well as the efficient and effective use of resources allocated to the health sector will help improve citizens' lives, population health, life expectancy, and labour force productivity.

A succinct suggestion therefore is the need for policymakers and other stakeholders in the health sector administration of the country to devote more attention to the industry, and release / increase its annual budgetary allocation as appropriate. Nevertheless, the key to excellent outcomes lies not in the usual increase of specific budget allocations, but in the implementation of a scheme of government finances that connects specific spending and income choices to the extent necessary and ensures that the assigned fund is used as transparently as possible.

The ill-formulation and poor implementation of primary health care policy programmes as well as the non-commitment on the part of the federal government in Nigeria to health sector development initiatives, amidst others duly relates to the emphasis made by some previous studies (Bakare et al., 2011; Abdulraheem et al., 2012; Ude et al., 2014;

Okoli et al., 2016; Ang et al., 2017) that in context of the Nigerian environment and other developing nations the practice and or delivery of primary health care services is still faced with major challenges and constraints of shortage of funds which as a result hamper its development, but active government support could yield substantial improvement. However, more emphasis need be placed on the capital expenditures on health as this will facilitate rapid development of the health sector.

Besides, as this article indicate that government spending on primary health care is essential to enhancing citizens' socio-economic well-being, health workers could be trained and retrained to be more efficient, and more workers (labor) could be recruited into the health sector in order to bring about development not only in the sector but in the economy as a whole. These will be in effort to address some of the human limitations identifiable in the delivery of health care services.

AFDB (2013) affirmed that reinforcing health care systems and ensuring equity in access to health services are particularly significant priorities for African countries' governments in the future. Moreover, AFDB et al. (2017) argue that bad health hazards have a possibly huge effect on harming productivity and hence development, which invariably indicates a powerful preventive case to invest in efficient health systems. Nonetheless, as the poor suffers the burden of ill health disproportionately, investing in health is both pro-poor and as such allows the development of a productive workforce.

Other recommendations also vital in addressing identifiable constraints in primary health care service delivery, more especially in Nigeria, include: (1) the tiers of government need help to facilitate an enabling environment for local and international agencies to ensure that comprehensive primary health care is practiced in the localities as against the selective primary health care which is not inclusive, (2) community-oriented health care programmes and policies should be fostered in all local government areas, and (3) the federal government could further empower and motivate health workers to carry out health education and training in rural communities, for proper understanding of the real benefit of primary health care, and also ensure proper implementation. In effect therefore, there is the call for top-down approach between government / policy makers and community stakeholders in strides for effort to ensure the development of the health sector, particularly in terms of achieving effective and efficient delivery / provision of primary health care services, and for such effort to be in part a panacea to attain inclusive growth.

Finally, as this article makes a case within the domain of (policy) implementation and health sector outcomes, further research could be to evaluate at the grass-root level the extent of accessibility and utilization of existing primary health care centres / facilities / services, in current time, to ascertain if still existent certain spatial, structural and or human constraints that undermine health sector outcomes and inevitably we attaining inclusive growth.

REFERENCES

Abdulraheem, I. S. Oladipo, A. R. & Amodu, M. O. (2012). Primary health care services in Nigeria: Critical Issues and Strategies for enhancing the use of the rural community. *Journal of Public Health and Epidemiology* 4(1): 5-13.

Abimbola S. (2012). How to improve the quality of primary healthcare in Nigeria. The BMJ Bloggs

Aigbiremolen, A. O, Alenoghena, I., Eboreime, E. & Abejegah, C. (2014). Primary health care in Nigeria: From conceptualization to implementation. *Journal of Medical and Applied Biosciences* 6 (2)

AfDB (2013). Health in Africa over the next 50 years. African Development Bank, Tunis

(https://www.afdb.org/fileadmin/uploads/afdb/Documents/Publications/Economic_Brief_-_Health_in_Africa_Over_the_Next_50_Years.pdf.)

AFDB, OECD & UNDP (2017). Africa economic outlook.

(https://www.afdb.org/fileadmin/uploads/afdb/Documents/Publications/AEO_2017_Report_Full_English.pdf)

Ang, A. N. A., Cruz, S. A. M. T. dela, Pural, H. L. M. & Rosete, M. A. L. (2017). The economic determinants of child mortality in the Philippines: A panel analysis of 16 regions. *Review of Integrative Business and Economic Research* 6(1):75-101

Anyanwu, J. C. & Erhijakpor, A. E. O. (2009). Health expenditures and health outcomes in Africa. *African Development Review* 21(2):400-33

Bakare, A. S. & Olubokun, S. (2011). Health care expenditure and economic growth in Nigeria: An empirical study. *Journal of Emerging Trend in Economics and Management Sciences (JETEMS)* 2(2):83-87

Berger, M. C. & Messer, J. (2002). Public financing of health expenditures, insurance and health outcomes. *Applied Economics* 34 (17):2105-2113

Bhatia, H. L. (2002). *Public finance.* Vikas Publishing

Brown, C. V. & Jackson, P M. (1990). *Public sector economics.* Blackwell Publishers

Filmer, D. & Prittchet, L. (2007). Child mortality and public spending on health: How much money matter? Policy Research Working Paper 1864 (Washington D.C., World Bank)

Herrera, S. & Pang, G. (2005). Efficiency of public spending in developing countries: An efficiency frontier approach. *World Bank Policy Research Working Paper* 3645, June 2005

Ichoku, H. E & Fonta, W. M (2006). The distributional impact of healthcare financing in Nigeria: A case study of Enugu state. PMMA Working Paper pp17: 3-22

Kress, D. H., Su, Y. & Wang, H. (2016). Assessment of primary health care system performance in Nigeria: Using the primary health care performance indicator conceptual framework. *Health System and Reforms* 2(4): 302

Musgrave, R. A & Musgrave, P. B. (1989). *Public finance in theory and practice.* New York, USA: McGraw-Hill

Nitti, F. S. (1903). *Principi di scienza delle finanzie* (https://archive.org/stream/principidiscienz00nittuoft#page/n5/mode/2up)

Nixon, J. & Ulmann, P. (2006). The relationship between health care expenditure and health outcomes. *The European Journal of Health Economics* 7(1):7-18

Novignon, J. Olakojo, S. A. & Nonvignon, J. (2012). The effects of public and private health care expenditure on health status in sub-Saharan Africa: New evidence from panel data analysis, *Health Economics Review* 2(22) (https://doi.org/10.1186/2191-1991-2-22)

Obalum, D. C & Fiberesima, F. (2012). Nigerian national health insurance scheme (NHIS): An overview. *Nigerian Postgraduate Medical Journal* 19(3):167-74

Odior, E. S (2011). Government expenditure on health, economic growth and long waves in a CGE micro-simulation analysis: The case of Nigeria. *European Journal of Economics, Finance and Administrative Sciences* 31(4) 1450-2275

Olise, P. (2012). *Primary health care for sustainable development. Abuja: Ozege Publications*

Oluwatobi, S. O. & Ogunrinola, O. I. (2011). Government expenditure on human capital development: Implications for economic growth in Nigeria. *Journal of Sustainable Development* 4(3) (http://dx.doi.org/10.5539/jsd.v4n3p72)

Okoli, U., Eze-Ajoku, E., Oludipe, M., Spieker, N., Ekezie, W. & Ohiri, K. (2016). Improving quality of care in primary health-care facilities in rural Nigeria: Successes and challenges. *Health Services Research and*

Managerial Epidemiology 3 (https://doi.org/10.1177/2333392816662581)

Saad, W. & KalaKech, K. (2009). The nature of government expenditure and its impact on sustainable economic growth. *Middle Eastern Finance and Economics* 4.

Sen, A. (1985). *Commodities and Capabilities*. North-Holland

Taiwo, O. A., Soyele, O. O., & Ndubuizu, G. U. (2014). Pattern of utilization of dental services at federal medical centre, Katsina, northwest Nigeria. *Sahel Medical Journal* 17(3): 108-11 (http://www.smjonline.org/text.asp?2014/17/3/108/140294)

Ude, D. K. & Ekesiobi, C. S. (2014). Effect of per capita health spending on child mortality in Nigeria. *International Journal of Innovative Research and Development* 3(9)

United Nations Department of Economic and Social Affairs (2015) Sustained and inclusive economic growth. Excerpt from Proceedings on Sustainable Development Knowledge Platform

Wagner, A. (1893). *Founding of political economy* (Third Edition), C. F. Winter (https://archive.org/details/grundlegungderp00wagngoog; https://archive.org/stream/grundlegungderp00wagngoog/grundlegungderp00wagngoog_djvu.txt; http://www.doiserbia.nb.rs/img/doi/1452-595X/2013/1452-595X1304457A.pdf)

World Health Organization-United Nations Children Fund (WHO-UNICEF) (1978). Declaration of Alma Ata.

World Health Organization - WHO (2011). The Abuja declaration: Ten years on. http://www.who.int/healthsystems/publications/abuja_report_aug_2011.pdf?

CONCLUDING THOUGHTS

So much more could be shared on the supposed pathway(s) to enhance the state of the health and education subsectors in Nigeria, and invariably for the improved welfare of the country's citizenry. This short piece surely would not be regarded as exhaustive, but one of many possibilities. Nonetheless, with some points highlighted, some suggestions raised and or put forth, amidst many succinct perspectives for the onward progress of these considered subsectors in Nigeria would be the need for continued collaboration of all sectoral stakeholders as well as an obvious stance and or commitment to a top-down approach to addressing the prevailing and challenging realities.

www.ingramcontent.com/pod-product-compliance
Lightning Source LLC
Chambersburg PA
CBHW030444220526
45464CB00006B/2408